D1315977

Science Matters
THE ROCK CYCLE

Melanie Ostopowich

WEIGL PUBLISHERS INC.

Published by Weigl Publishers Inc.
350 5th Avenue, Suite 3304, PMB 6G
New York, NY USA 10118-0069
Web site: www.weigl.com
Copyright 2005 WEIGL PUBLISHERS INC.
All rights reserved. No part of this publication may be reproduced, stored in a retrieval system, or transmitted in any form or by any means, electronic, mechanical, photocopying, recording, or otherwise, without the prior written permission of the publisher.

Library of Congress Cataloging-in-Publication Data

Ostopowich, Melanie.
  The rock cycle / Melanie Ostopowich.
      p. cm. -- (Science matters)
  Includes index.
  ISBN 1-59036-209-8 (lib. bdg. : alk. paper) ISBN 1-59036-251-9 (softcover)
  1. Petrology--Juvenile literature. I. Title. II. Series.
  QE432.2.O86 2005
  552--dc22

                        2004004133

Printed in the United States of America
1 2 3 4 5 6 7 8 9 0   08 07 06 05 04

Project Coordinator Tina Schwartzenberger **Copy Editor** Heather Kissock
Design Terry Paulhus **Layout** Bryan Pezzi
Photo Researcher Ellen Bryan

Photograph Credits

Every reasonable effort has been made to trace ownership and to obtain permission to reprint copyright material. The publishers would be pleased to have any errors or omissions brought to their attention so that they may be corrected in subsequent printings.

Cover: Bryce Canyon National Park, Utah from Tom Stack & Associates (Mark Newman)
Corel Corporation: pages 15, 16; **Mary Evans Picture Library:** page 19; **Martin Miller:** page 10; **Bryan Pezzi:** pages 7, 12-13; **Photos.com:** pages 1, 3T, 3M, 3B, 4, 8, 9, 11, 14, 17, 18, 22T, 22B, 23T, 23B; **United States Geological Survey:** page 6 (J.D. Griggs).

Contents

Studying the Rock Cycle

Rocks form over time. As time passes, rocks change from one type to another. This process is called the rock cycle.

The rock cycle never ends. Rocks are always changing. The rock cycle is a slow process that **recycles** rocks. The material that makes up rocks is not destroyed. It changes from one type of rock to another.

■ Rocks are found all over Earth. Mountains are rocks. Rocks make up the ocean floor. Rocks also form coastlines.

Rock Cycle Facts

From mountains to ocean floors, Earth is made of rock. Read on to learn interesting facts about the rock cycle.

- The rocks on Earth today are made from the same material as the rocks on Earth when dinosaurs lived. The rocks have changed, but the material they are made from has not.

- There are many different types of rocks. No two rocks are the same.

- The rock cycle takes millions of years to complete.

- Earth's surface is constantly moving. It moves about as fast as human fingernails grow.

- Geology is the science that studies Earth's **structure**. Geologists study rocks, mountains, and cliffs to learn what Earth is made from. They also study how Earth has changed over time.

Drift Away

Earth's surface is made of a thin layer of rock called the **crust**. The crust is broken into twelve large pieces called tectonic plates. A river of hot **magma** flows under the plates. The movement of the magma causes the plates to slowly shift. Sometimes the plates move away from each other. Other times they hit against each other. This movement is what causes mountains, volcanoes, and earthquakes.

■ When magma erupts from volcanoes, it is called lava.

Supercontinent

The map of Earth is always changing. It changes because the tectonic plates are always moving.

About 225 million years ago, all the **continents** were one giant land mass. This was a supercontinent called *Pangaea*. About 200 million years ago, Pangaea broke apart. This happened very slowly. The pieces began drifting away from each other. Oceans filled the spaces between continents. Now, each continent sits on a separate plate. The plates and the continents are still moving.

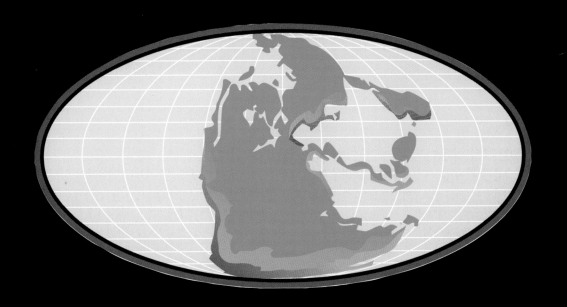

Sedimentary Rocks

Water, wind, and ice scatter sediments, which are very small pieces of rock and dirt. Sedimentary rock forms when layers of sediments build up. The weight of many layers of sediment causes them to harden. Water in spaces between grains of sediment cements the sediment together.

Geologists group sedimentary rock in three ways. Clastic rocks are formed from broken pieces of existing rocks and **minerals**. Chemical rocks form when minerals mix with water, usually sea water or lake water, to form a solid. Organic rocks form from animal and plant remains. It is common for sedimentary rocks to contain all three types of sediment.

■ Shale is a sedimentary rock formed mostly from clay. Fossils, the rocklike remains of plants and animals, can be found in shale.

Igneous Rocks

Igneous rocks are the oldest type of rock. They are also the strongest type of rock. Granite is an igneous rock. It is used to make buildings. Basalt is also an igneous rock. It is used to make roads.

The word "igneous" comes from a Greek word that means fire-formed. What is another word similar to igneous that means to start a fire?

Answer: ignite

Metamorphic Rocks

Metamorphic rocks form when igneous and sedimentary rocks change. Igneous and sedimentary rocks can be exposed to high levels of heat and pressure in Earth's crust. This heat and pressure cause the rock to change into a new type of rock. The new type of rock is called metamorphic. The rock that changes is called the parent rock. The texture of the parent rock changes when metamorphic rock forms. The minerals inside the rock also change.

● Metamorphic rocks are the least common type of rock.

Stress, Heat, and Pressure

Stress, heat, and pressure can make one type of rock change into a new kind of rock. This process takes a long time.

Rocks are made from minerals. Stress, heat, and pressure cause minerals in rocks to bend, crack, and even snap. These kinds of changes create metamorphic rocks.

The temperature is higher deep inside Earth. Molten rock can bake other rocks. Rocks exposed to this heat adjust to become more stable under the new higher temperature and pressure.

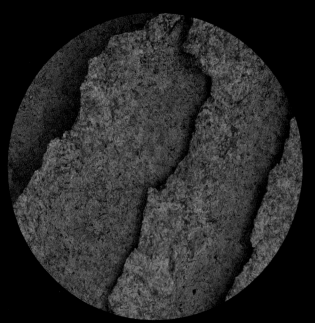

● Shale is a sedimentary rock. When it is squeezed and heated deep inside Earth, it can turn into slate, a metamorphic rock.

The Rock Cycle

The process in which rocks form, break down, and reform is called the rock cycle. It takes thousands of years for one rock to change.

Over time, all types of rocks break apart and become sediments. Weathering causes sediments to gather and pile up. Pressure pushes the sediments together. This creates sedimentary rock.

High temperature and pressure change sedimentary and igneous rocks into metamorphic rocks. Heat and pressure also cause rock to melt. New igneous rocks form from cooled lava.

Sedimentary Rocks

Metamorphic Rocks

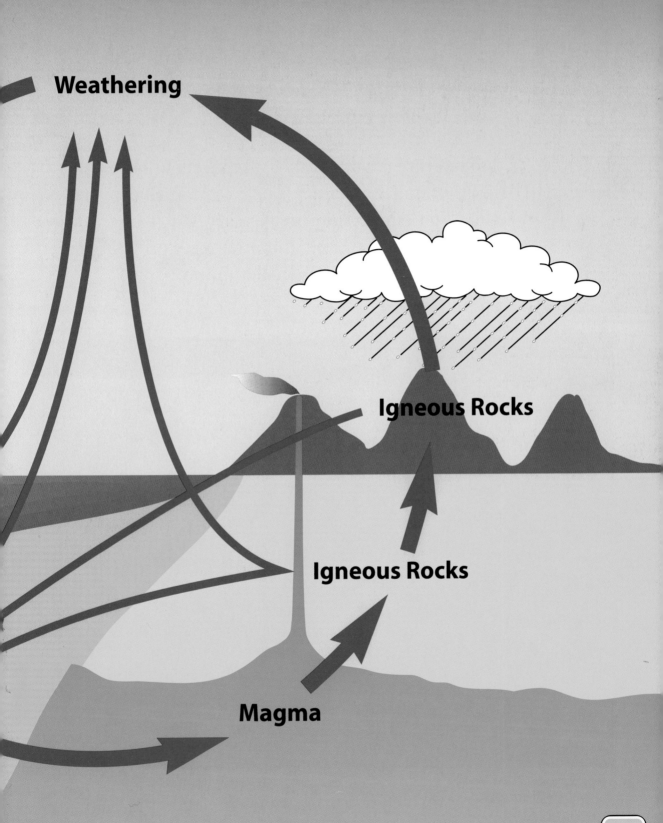

Weathering

Igneous Rocks

Igneous Rocks

Magma

Weathering Rocks

Rocks on Earth's surface are exposed to sunshine, rain, wind, ice, and heat. Over time, these elements slowly break down rocks. This is called weathering.

Temperature changes cause all objects to become slightly smaller or larger. Rocks cannot change size easily. Sometimes they break apart. Water in cracks inside a rock can freeze and melt. This process can make a rock break into smaller pieces.

● Rocks on high ridges resist weathering better than surrounding rocks.

Rocks and Erosion

Weathering is one way rocks can be broken down. Another way is erosion. Weathering and erosion are part of the rock cycle.

Erosion has created beautiful landforms all over the world. The Grand Canyon is a good example. The Colorado River flows through the lowest part of the Grand Canyon. Over 6 million years, the river has eroded the canyon.

The Colorado River cuts into the rock. The river erodes rock on the sides and bottom of the canyon. As the rock wears away, the water level in the river drops and continues to erode layers of newly-exposed rock at the bottom of the river. This process of erosion continues today.

Sediments

Weathering and erosion cause rocks to break into small pieces called sediments. Wind and water easily move sediments across land and through rivers and streams. Sediments eventually stop moving and settle, usually at the bottom of rivers and lakes. Over time, layers of sediments pile up. The weight of the layers causes the sediments to become tightly stuck together and form sedimentary rock. Weathering then breaks the rock apart again. The rock cycle repeats itself.

Sediment builds up in lakes, oceans, and rivers. Of the rocks on Earth's surface, 70 to 75 percent are sedimentary.

Fossils

A fossil is the rocklike remains of a plant or animal. Fossils are usually found in sedimentary rock.

The remains of plants and animals are sometimes trapped in layers of sediment. When sediments turn into sedimentary rocks, the remains are preserved inside them. These remains are called fossils. Fossils tell scientists what life was like on Earth long ago.

▪ The heat and pressure that create igneous and sedimentary rocks destroy fossils.

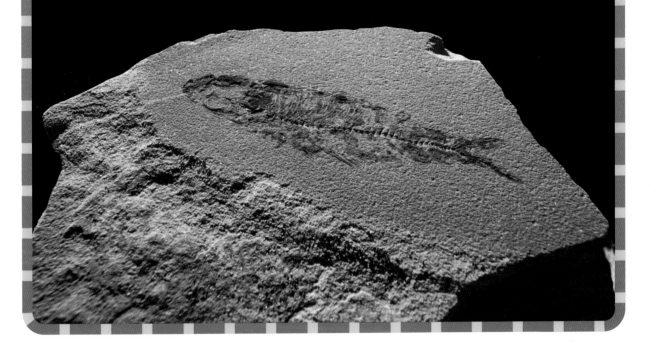

Rock Recycling

Rocks are the ultimate recyclers. The rock on a lakeshore could have been part of a huge mountain at one time. A caveman could even have stepped on it.

Rocks are formed and recycled through the movement of tectonic plates. The same movement that creates mountains, volcanoes, and earthquakes also causes rocks to break down. Rocks are recycled when pieces of old rocks become part of new rocks.

● Wind and water wear away rock over millions of years. This process creates formations such as this natural bridge.

A Life of Science

James Hutton

James Hutton, an 18th-century Scottish farmer, was the first person to recognize the rock cycle. He saw that weather was eroding his field. However, the **soil** was not disappearing completely. He realized there must be a way that the soil was replacing itself. He thought Earth was lifting up and producing new soil surfaces. We now know this is not true.

James Hutton also saw a connection between the three types of rock. He wrote a book about his theories on the rock cycle.

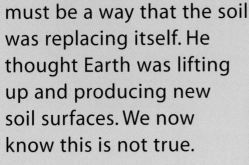

Surfing Our Earth

How can I find more information about the rock cycle?

- Libraries have many interesting books about the rock cycle.
- Science centers and museums are great places to learn about the rock cycle.
- The Internet offers some great Web sites dedicated to the rock cycle.

Where can I find a good reference Web site to learn more about the rock cycle?

Encarta Homepage
www.encarta.com

- Type any rock-related term into the search engine. Some terms to try include "rock cycle" and "erosion."

How can I find out more about the rock cycle, rocks, and fossils?

Windows to the Universe
www.windows.ucar.edu

- Click on "Geology" to learn how rocks are made and destroyed. You can also learn about minerals and fossils.

Science in Action

You can create your own sandstone rock. You will need:

- 1 large measuring cup
- 1 1/2 cups (355 mL) fine-grained sand
- 1 1/4 cups (296 mL) plaster of Paris
- 1 1/4 cups (296 mL) water
- 2 quart (2 L) plastic bottle
- scissors
- wooden spoon

Carefully cut the plastic bottle in half.

Pour the sand into the bottle. Add the plaster of Paris to the sand in the bottle. Use the spoon, and mix very well.

Slowly add water to the sand and plaster of Paris mixture. Mix carefully while still adding water. Clean up any plaster that spills or splatters. Plaster becomes rock hard when it dries.

Leave the mixture to set overnight.

The next day, cut the plastic away from the sandstone. What kind of rock have you created? Is it igneous, metamorphic, or sedimentary?

What Have You Learned?

1 What do geologists study?

2 Name five things that cause rocks to change.

3 Who was James Hutton?

4 What was the name of the giant land mass from which the continents formed?

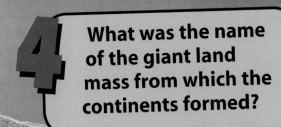

5 What process created the Grand Canyon?

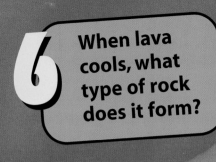

6 When lava cools, what type of rock does it form?

7 What type of rock is formed from another rock changing form?

8 What kind of rock forms from sediments pressed together?

9 What is weathering?

10 In what type of rock will you most often find fossils?

Answers: 1. Geologists study Earth's structure. **2.** Stress, heat, pressure, weathering, and erosion can cause rocks to change. **3.** James Hutton was a Scottish farmer who first recognized the rock cycle. **4.** Pangaea **5.** Erosion **6.** Igneous **7.** Metamorphic **8.** Sedimentary **9.** Weathering is the slow process of sunshine, rain, wind, ice, and heat breaking down rocks. **10.** Sedimentary

Words to Know

continents: the seven large land areas on Earth, namely Asia, Africa, Europe, North America, South America, Antarctica, and Australia

crust: Earth's hard, top layer

erosion: the removal of rock and pieces of soil by natural forces such as running water, ice, waves, and wind

igneous rocks: rocks formed when magma, or molten rock, cools

magma: melted rock material under Earth's crust

minerals: natural substances that are not an animal or plant

recycles: reuses materials

soil: tiny pieces of rock that form the top layer of the ground in which plants grow

stress: force or strain put on an object by another object

structure: the way the parts that make something are arranged

Index